The Story of My Misfortunes

The Autobiography of Peter Abelard

Translated by Henry Adams Bellows

Published by Pantianos Classics

ISBN-13: 978-1979548113

This translation was first published in 1922

Contents

Foreword

OFTEN the hearts of men and women are stirred, as likewise they are soothed in their sorrows more by example than by words. And therefore, because I too I have known some consolation from speech had with one who was a witness thereof, am I now minded to write of the sufferings which have sprung out of my misfortunes, for the eyes of one who, though absent, is of himself ever a consoler. This I do so that, in comparing your sorrows with mine, you may discover that yours are in truth nought, or at the most but of small account, and so shall you come to bear them more easily.

Chapter One - Of the Birthplace of Pierre Abelard and of His Parents

KNOW, then, that I am come from a certain town which was built on the way into lesser Brittany, distant some eight miles, as I think, eastward from the city of Nantes, and in its own tongue called Palets. Such is the nature of that country, or, it may be, of them who dwell there—for in truth they are quick in fancy—that my mind bent itself easily to the study of letters. Yet more, I had a father who had won some smattering of letters before he had girded on the soldier's belt. And so it came about that long afterwards his love thereof was so strong that he saw to it that each son of his should be taught in letters even earlier than in the management of arms. Thus indeed did it come to pass. And because I was his first born, and for that reason the more dear to him, he sought with double diligence to have me wisely taught. For my part, the more I went forward in the study of letters, and ever more easily, the greater became the ardour of my devotion to them, until in truth I was so enthralled by my passion for learning that, gladly leaving to my brothers the pomp of glory in arms, the right of heritage and all the honours that should have been mine as the eldest born, I fled utterly from the court of Mars that I might win learning in the bosom of Minerva. And—since I found the armory of logical reasoning more to my liking than the other forms of philosophy, I exchanged all other weapons for these, and to the prizes of victory in war I preferred the battle of minds in disputation. Thenceforth, journeying through many provinces, and debating as I went, going whithersoever I heard that the study of my chosen art most flourished, I became such an one as the Peripatetics.

Chapter Two - Of the Persecution He Had from His Master William of Champeaux

OF HIS ADVENTURES AT MELUN, AT CORBEIL AND AT PARIS, HIS WITHDRAWAL FROM THE CITY OF THE PARISIANS TO MELUN, AND HIS RETURN TO MONT STE GENEVIEVE, OF HIS JOURNEY TO HIS OLD HOME

I CAME at length to Paris, where above all in those days the art of dialectics was most flourishing, and there did I meet William of Champeaux, my teacher, a man most distinguished in his science both by his renown and by his true merit. With him I remained for some time, at first indeed well liked of him; but later I brought him great grief, because I undertook to refute certain of his opinions, not infrequently attacking him in disputation, and now and then in these debates I was adjudged victor. Now this, to those among my fellow students who were ranked foremost, seemed all the more insufferable because of my youth and the brief duration of my studies.

Out of this sprang the beginning of my misfortunes, which have followed me even to the present day; the more widely my fame was spread abroad, the more bitter was the envy that was kindled against me. It was given out that I, presuming on my gifts far beyond the warranty of my youth, was aspiring despite my tender years to the leadership of a school; nay, more, that I was making ready the very place in which I would undertake this task, the place being none other than the castle of Melun, at that time a royal seat. My teacher himself had some foreknowledge of this, and tried to remove my school as far as possible from his own. Working in secret, he sought in every way he could before I left his following to bring to nought the school I had planned and the place I had chosen for It. Since, however, in that very place he had many rivals, and some of them men of influence among the great ones of the land, relying on their aid I won to the fulfillment of my wish; the support of many was secured for me by reason of his own unconcealed envy. From this small inception of my school, my fame in the art of dialectics began to spread abroad, so that little by little the renown, not alone of those who had been my fellow students, but of our very teacher himself, grew dim and was like to die out altogether. Thus it came about that, still more confident in myself, I moved my school as soon as I well might to the castle of Corbeil, which is hard by the city of Paris, for there I knew there would be given more frequent chance for my assaults in our battle of disputation.

No long time thereafter I was smitten with a grievous illness, brought upon me by my immoderate zeal for study. This illness forced me to turn homeward to my native province, and thus for some years I was as if cut off from France. And yet, for that very reason, I was sought out all the more eagerly by those whose hearts were troubled by the lore of dialectics. But after a few years had passed, and I was whole again from my sickness, I learned that my teacher, that same William Archdeacon of Paris, had changed his former garb and joined an order of the regular clergy. This he had done, or so men said, in order that he might be deemed more deeply religious, and so might be elevated to a loftier rank in the prelacy, a thing which, in truth, very soon came to pass, for he was made bishop of Chalons. Nevertheless, the garb he had donned by reason of his conversion did nought to keep him away either from the city of Paris or from his wonted study of philosophy; and in the very monastery wherein he had shut himself up for the sake of religion he straightway set to teaching again after the same fashion as before.

To him did I return for I was eager to learn more of rhetoric from his lips; and in the course of our many arguments on various matters, I compelled him by most potent reasoning first to alter his former opinion on the subject of the universals, and finally to abandon it altogether. Now, the basis of this old concept of his regarding the reality of universal ideas was that the same quality formed the essence alike of the abstract whole and of the individuals which were its parts: in other words, that there could be no essential differences among these individuals, all being alike save for such variety as might grow out of the many accidents of existence. Thereafter, however, he corrected this opinion, no longer maintaining that the same quality was the essence of all things, but that, rather, it manifested itself in them through diverse ways. This problem of universals is ever the most vexed one among logicians, to such a degree, indeed, that even Porphyry, writing in his "Isagoge" regarding universals, dared not attempt a final pronouncement thereon, saying rather: "This is the deepest of all problems of its kind." Wherefore it followed that when William had first revised and then finally abandoned altogether his views on this one sub-

ject, his lecturing sank into such a state of negligent reasoning that it could scarce be called lecturing on the science of dialectics at all; it was as if all
his science had been bound up in this one question
of the nature of universals.

Thus it came about that my teaching won such
strength and authority that even those who before
had clung most vehemently to my former master,
and most bitterly attacked my doctrines, now
flocked to my school. The very man who had succeeded to my master's chair in the Paris school offered me his post, in order that he might put himself under my tutelage along with all the rest, and
this in the very place where of old his master and
mine had reigned. And when, in so short a time, my
master saw me directing the study of dialectics
there, it is not easy to find words to tell with what
envy he was consumed or with what pain he was
tormented. He could not long, in truth, bear the an-
guish of what he felt to be his wrongs, and shrewd-
ly he attacked me that he might drive me forth.
And because there was nought in my conduct
whereby he could come at me openly, he tried to
steal away the school by launching the vilest cal-
umnies against him who had yielded his post to
me, and by putting in his place a certain rival of
mine. So then I returned to Melun, and set up my
school there as before; and the more openly his

envy pursued me, the greater was the authority it conferred upon me. Even so held the poet: "Jealousy aims at the peaks; the winds storm the loftiest summits." (Ovid:"Remedy for Love," I,369.)

Not long thereafter, when William became aware of the fact that almost all his students were holding grave doubts as to his religion, and were whispering earnestly among themselves about his conversion, deeming that he had by no means abandoned this world, he withdrew himself and his brotherhood, together with his students, to a certain estate far distant from the city. Forthwith I returned from Melun to Paris, hoping for peace from him in the future. But since, as I have said, he had caused my place to be occupied by a rival of mine, I pitched the camp, as it were, of my school outside the city on Mont Ste. Genevieve. Thus I was as one laying siege to him who had taken possession of my post. No sooner had my master heard of this than he brazenly returned post haste to the city, bringing back with him such students as he could, and reinstating his brotherhood in their former monastery, much as if he would free his soldiery, whom he had deserted, from my blockade. In truth, though, if it was his purpose to bring them succour, he did nought but hurt them. Before that time my rival had indeed had a certain number of students, of one sort and another, chiefly by reason of his lectures on Priscian, in which he was considered of great authority. After our master had returned, however, he lost nearly all of these followers, and thus was compelled to give up the direction of the school. Not long thereafter, apparently despairing further of worldly fame, he was converted to the monastic life.

Following the return of our master to the city, the combats in disputation which my scholars waged both with him himself and with his pupils, and the successes which fortune gave to us, and above all to me, in these wars, you have long since learned of through your own experience. The boast of Ajax, though I speak it more temperately, I still am bold enough to make:

> *"if fain you would learn now*
> *How victory crowned the battle, by him was*
> *I never vanquished."*
> **- (Ovid , "Metamorphoses," XIII, 89.)**

But even were I to be silent, the fact proclaims itself, and its outcome reveals the truth regarding it.

While these things were happening, it became needful for me again to repair to my old home, by reason of my dear mother, Lucia, for after the conversion of my father, Berengarius, to the monastic life, she so ordered her affairs as to do likewise. When all this had been completed, I returned to France, above all in order that I might study theology, since now my oft-mentioned teacher, William, was active in the episcopate of Chalons. In this field of learning Anselm of Laon, who was his teacher therein, had for long years enjoyed the greatest renown.

Chapter Three - Of How He Came to Laon to Seek Anselm As Teacher

I SOUGHT out, therefore, this same venerable man, whose fame, in truth, was more the result of long established custom than of the potency of his own talent or intellect. If any one came to him impelled by doubt on any subject, he went away more doubtful still. He was wonderful, indeed, in the eyes of these who only listened to him, but those who asked him questions perforce held him as nought. He had a miraculous flow of words, but they were contemptible in meaning and quite void of reason. When he kindled a fire, he filled his house with smoke and illumined it not at all. He was a tree which seemed noble to those who gazed upon its leaves from afar, but to those who came nearer and examined it more closely was revealed its barrenness. When, therefore, I had come to this tree that I might pluck the fruit thereof, I discovered that it was indeed the fig tree which Our Lord cursed (Matthew xxi. 19; Mark xi. 13), or that ancient oak to which Lucan likened Pompey, saying:

"he stands, the shade of a name once mighty,
Like to the towering oak in the midst of the
fruitful field."

- (Lucan, "Pharsalia," IV, 135-)

It was not long before I made this discovery, and stretched myself lazily in the shade of that same tree. I went to his lectures less and less often, a thing which some among his eminent followers took sorely to heart, because they interpreted it as a mark of contempt for so illustrious a teacher. Thenceforth they secretly sought !to influence him against me, and by their vile insinuations made me hated of him. It chanced, moreover, that one day, after the exposition of certain texts, we scholars were jesting among ourselves, and one of them, seeking to draw me out, asked me what I thought of the lectures on the Books of Scripture. I, who had as yet studied only the sciences, replied that following such lectures seemed to me most useful in so far as the salvation of the soul was concerned, but that it appeared quite extraordinary to me that educated persons should not be able to understand the sacred books simply by studying them themselves, together with the glosses thereon, and without the aid of any teacher. Most of those who were present mocked at me, and asked whether I myself could do as I had said, or whether I would dare to undertake it. I answered that if they wished, I was ready to try it. Forthwith they cried out and jeered all the more. "Well and good," said they; "we agree to the test. Pick out and give us an exposition of some doubtful passage in the Scriptures, I so that we can put this boast of yours to the proof." And they all chose that most obscure prophecy of Ezekiel.

I accepted the challenge, and invited them to attend a lecture on the very next day. Whereupon they undertook to give me good advice, saying that I should by no means make undue haste in so important a matter, but that I ought to devote a much longer space to working out my exposition and offsetting my inexperience by diligent toil. To this I replied indignantly that it was my wont to win success, not by routine, but by ability. I added that I would abandon the test altogether unless they would agree not to put off their attendance at my lecture. In truth at this first lecture of mine only a few were present, for it seemed quite absurd to all of them that I. hitherto so inexperienced in discussing the Scriptures, should attempt the thing so hastily. However, this lecture gave such satisfaction to all those who heard it that they spread its praises abroad with notable enthusiasm, and thus compelled me to continue my interpretation of the sacred text. When word of this was bruited about, those who had stayed away from the first lecture came eagerly, some to the second and more to the third, and all of them were eager to write down the glosses which I had begun on the first day, so as to have them from the very beginning.

Chapter Four - Of the Persecution He Had from His Teacher Anselm

NOW this venerable man of whom I have spoken was acutely smitten with envy, and straightway incited, as I have already mentioned, by the insinuations of sundry persons, began to persecute me for my lecturing on the Scriptures no less bitterly than my former master, William, had done for my work in philosophy. At that time there were in this old man's school two who were considered far to excel all the others: Alberic of Rheims and Lotulphe the Lombard. The better opinion these two held of themselves, the more they were incensed against me. Chiefly at their suggestion, as it afterwards transpired, yonder venerable coward had the impudence to forbid me to carry on any further in his school the work of preparing glosses which I had thus begun. The pretext he alleged was that if by chance in the course of this work I should write anything containing blunders—as was likely enough in view of my lack of training—the thing might be imputed to him. When this came to the ears of his scholars, they were filled with indignation at so undisguised a manifestation of spite, the like of which had never been directed against any one before. The more obvious this rancour became, the more it redounded to my honour, and his persecution did nought save to make me more famous.

Chapter Five - Of How He Returned to Paris and Finished the Glosses Which He Had Begun at Laon

AND so, after a few days, I returned to Paris, and there for several years I peacefully directed the school which formerly had been destined for me, nay, even offered to me, but from which I had been driven out. At the very outset of my work there, I set about completing the glosses on Ezekiel which I had begun at Laon. These proved so satisfactory to all who read them that they came to believe me no less adept in lecturing on theology than I had proved myself to be in the field of philosophy. Thus my school was notably increased in size by reason of my lectures on subjects of both these kinds, and the amount of financial profit as well as glory which it brought me cannot be concealed from you, for the matter talked of. But prosperity always puffs up the foolish and worldly comfort enervates the soul, rendering it an easy prey to carnal temptations. Thus I who by this time had come to regard myself as the only philosopher remaining in the whole world, and had ceased to fear any further disturbance of my peace, began to loosen the rein on my desires, although hitherto I had always lived in the utmost continence. And the greater progress I made in my lecturing on philosophy or theology, the more I departed alike from the practice of the philosophers and the spirit of the divines in the uncleanness of my life. For it is well known, methinks, that philosophers, and still more those who have devoted their lives to arousing the love of sacred study, have been strong above all else in the beauty of chastity.

Thus did it come to pass that while I was utterly absorbed in pride and sensuality, divine grace, the cure for both diseases, was forced upon me, even though I, forsooth would fain have shunned it. First was I punished for my sensuality, and then for my pride. For my sensuality I lost those things whereby I practiced it; for my pride, engendered in me by my knowledge of letters and it is even as the Apostle said: "Knowledge puffeth itself up" (I Cor. viii. 1)—I knew the humiliation of seeing burned the very book in which I most gloried. And now it is my desire that you should know the stories of these two happenings, understanding them more truly from learning the very facts than from hearing what is spoken of them, and in the order in which they came about. Because I had ever held in abhorrence the foulness of prostitutes, because I had diligently kept myself from all excesses and from association with the women of noble birth who attended the school, because I knew so little of the common talk of ordinary people, perverse and subtly flattering chance gave birth to an occasion for casting me lightly down from the heights of my own exaltation. Nay, in such case not even divine goodness could redeem one who, having been so proud, was brought to such shame, were it not for the blessed gift of grace.

Chapter Six - Of How, Brought Low by His Love for Heloise, He Was Wounded in Body and Soul

NOW there dwelt in that same city of Paris a certain young girl named Heloise, the neice of a canon who was called Fulbert. Her uncle's love for her was equalled only by his desire that she should have the best education which he could possibly procure for her. Of no mean beauty, she stood out above all by reason of her abundant knowledge of letters. Now this virtue is rare among women, and for that very reason it doubly graced the maiden, and made her the most worthy of renown in the entire kingdom. It was this young girl whom I, after carefully considering all those qualities which are wont to attract lovers, determined to unite with myself in the bonds of love, and indeed the thing seemed to me very easy to be done. So distinguished was my name, and I possessed such advantages of youth and comeliness, that no matter what woman I might favour with my love, I dreaded rejection of none. Then, too, I believed that I could win the maiden's consent all the more easily by reason of her knowledge of letters and her zeal therefor; so, even if we were parted, we might yet be together in thought with the aid of written messages. Perchance, too, we might be able to write more boldly than we could speak, and thus at all times could we live in joyous intimacy.

Thus, utterly aflame with my passion for this maiden, I sought to discover means whereby I might have daily and familiar speech with her, thereby the more easily to win her consent. For this purpose I persuaded the girl's uncle, with the aid of some of his friends to take me into his household—for he dwelt hard by my school—in return for the payment of a small sum. My pretext for this was that the care of my own household was a serious handicap to my studies, and likewise burdened me with an expense far greater than I could afford. Now he was a man keen in avarice and likewise he was most desirous for his niece that her study of letters should ever go forward, so, for these two reasons I easily won his consent to the fulfillment of my wish, for he was fairly agape for my money, and at the same time believed that his niece would vastly benefit by my teaching. More even than this, by his own earnest entreaties he fell in with my desires beyond anything I had dared to hope, opening the way for my love; for he entrusted her wholly to my guidance, begging me to give her instruction whensoever I might be free from the duties of my school, no matter whether by day or by night, and to punish her sternly if ever I should find her negligent of her tasks. In all this the man's simplicity was nothing short of astounding to me; I should not have been more smitten with wonder if he had entrusted a tender lamb to the care of a ravenous wolf. When he had thus given her into my charge, not alone to be taught but even to be disciplined, what had he done save to give free scope to my desires, and to offer me every opportunity, even if I had not sought it, to bend her to my will with threats and blows if I failed to do so with caresses? There were, however, two things which particularly served to allay any foul suspicion: his own love for his niece, and my former reputation for continence.

Why should I say more? We were united first in the dwelling that sheltered our love, and then in the hearts that burned with it. Under the pretext of study we spent our hours in the happiness of love, and learning held out to us the secret opportunities that our passion craved. Our speech was more of love than of the books which lay open before us; our kisses far outnumbered our reasoned words. Our hands sought less the book than each other's bosoms—love drew our eyes together far more than the lesson drew them to the pages of our text. In order that there might be no suspicion, there were, indeed, sometimes blows, but love gave them, not anger; they were the marks, not of wrath, but of a tenderness surpassing the most fragrant balm in sweetness. What followed? No degree in love's progress was left untried by our passion, and if love itself could imagine any wonder as yet unknown, we discovered it. And our inexperience of such delights made us all the more ardent in our pursuit of them, so that our thirst for one another was still unquenched.

In measure as this passionate rapture absorbed me more and more, I devoted ever less time to philosophy and to the work of the school. Indeed it became loathsome to me to go to the school or to linger there; the labour, moreover, was very burdensome, since my nights were vigils of love and my days of study. My lecturing became utterly careless and lukewarm; I did nothing because of inspiration, but everything merely as a matter of habit. I had become nothing more than a reciter of my former discoveries, and though I still wrote poems, they dealt with love, not with the secrets of philosophy. Of these songs you yourself well know how some have become widely known and have been sung in many lands, chiefly, methinks, by those who delighted in the things of this world. As for the sorrow, the groans, the lamentations of my students when they perceived the preoccupation, nay, rather the chaos, of my mind, it is hard even to imagine them.

A thing so manifest could deceive only a few, no one, methinks, save him whose shame it chiefly bespoke, the girl's uncle, Fulbert. The truth was often enough hinted to him, and by many persons, but he could not believe it, partly, as I have said, by reason of his boundless love for his niece, and partly because of the well-known continence of my previous life. Indeed we do not easily suspect shame in those whom we most cherish, nor can there be the blot of foul suspicion on devoted love. Of this St. Jerome in his epistle to Sabinianus (Epist. 48) says: "We are wont to be the last to know the evils of our own households, and to be ignorant of the sins of our children and our wives, though our neighbours sing them aloud." But no matter how slow a matter may be in disclosing itself, it is sure to come forth at last, nor is it easy to hide from one what is known to all. So, after the lapse of several months, did it happen with us. Oh, how great was the uncle's grief when he learned the truth, and how bitter was the sorrow of the lovers when we were forced to part! With what shame was I overwhelmed, with what contrition smitten because of the blow which had fallen on her I loved, and what a tempest of misery burst over her by reason of my disgrace! Each grieved most, not for himself, but for the other. Each sought to allay, not his own sufferings, but those of the one he loved. The very sundering of our bodies served but to link our souls closer together; the plentitude of the love which was denied to us inflamed us more than ever. Once the first wildness of shame had passed, it left us more shameless than before, and as shame died within us the cause of it seemed to us ever more desirable. And so it chanced with us as, in the stories that the poets tell, it once happened with Mars and Venus when they were caught together.

It was not long after this that Heloise found that she was pregnant, and of this she wrote to me in the utmost exultation, at the same time asking me to consider what had best be done. Accordingly, on a night when her uncle was absent, we carried out the plan we had determined on, and I stole her secretly away from her uncle's house, sending her without delay to my own country. She remained there with my sister until she gave birth to a son, whom she named Astrolabe. Meanwhile her uncle after his return, was almost mad with grief; only one who had then seen him could rightly guess the burning agony of his sorrow and the bitterness of his shame. What steps to take against me, or what snares to set for me, he did not know. If he should kill me or do me some bodily hurt, he feared greatly lest his dear-loved niece should be made to suffer for it among my kinsfolk. He had no power to seize me and imprison me somewhere against my will, though I make no doubt he would have done so quickly enough had he been able or dared, for I had taken measures to guard against any such attempt.

At length, however, in pity for his boundless grief, and bitterly blaming myself for the suffering which my love had brought upon him through the baseness of the deception I had practiced, I went to him to entreat his forgiveness, promising to make any amends that he himself might decree. I pointed out that what had happened could not seem incredible to any one who had ever felt the power of love, or who remembered how, from the very beginning of the human race, women had cast down even the noblest men to utter ruin. And in order to make amends even beyond his extremest hope, I offered to marry her whom I had seduced, provided only the thing could be kept secret, so that I might suffer no loss of reputation thereby. To this he gladly assented, pledging his own faith and that of his kindred, and sealing with kisses the pact which I had sought of him—and all this that he might the more easily betray me.

Chapter Seven - Of the Arguments of Heloise Against Wedlock

OF HOW NONE THE LESS HE MADE HER HIS WIFE

FORTHWITH I repaired to my own country, and brought back thence my mistress, that I might make her my wife. She, however, most violently disapproved of this, and for two chief reasons: the danger thereof, and the disgrace which it would bring upon me. She swore that her uncle would never be appeased by such satisfaction as this, as, indeed, afterwards proved only too true. She asked how she could ever glory in me if she should make me thus inglorious, and should shame herself along with me. What penalties, she said, would the world rightly demand of her if she should rob it of so shining a light! What curses would follow such a loss to the Church, what tears among the philosophers would result from such a marriage! How unfitting, how lamentable it would be for me, whom nature had made for the whole world, to devote myself to one woman solely, and to subject myself to such humiliation! She vehemently rejected this marriage, which she felt would be in every way ignominious and burdensome to me.

Besides dwelling thus on the disgrace to me, she reminded me of the hardships of married life, to the avoidance of which the Apostle exhorts us, saying: "Art thou loosed from a wife? seek not a wife. But and marry, thou hast not sinned; and if a virgin marry she hath not sinned. Nevertheless such shall have trouble in the flesh: but I spare you" (I Cor. vii. 27). And again: "But I would have you to be free from cares" (I Cor. vii. 32). But if I would heed neither the counsel of the Apostle nor the exhortations of the saints regarding this heavy yoke of matrimony, she bade me at least consider the advice of the philosophers, and weigh carefully what had been written on this subject either by them or concerning their lives. Even the saints themselves have often and earnestly spoken on this subject for the purpose of warning us. Thus St. Jerome, in his first book against Jovinianus, makes Theophrastus set forth in great detail the intolerable annoyances and the endless disturbances of married life,

demonstrating with the most convincing arguments that no wise man should ever have a wife,
and concluding his reasons for this philosophic ex-
hortation with these words: "Who among Christians would not be overwhelmed by such arguments as these advanced by Theophrastus?"

Again, in the same work, St. Jerome tells how
Cicero, asked by Hircius after his divorce of Teren-
tia whether he would marry the sister of Hircius,
replied that he would do no such thing, saying that
he could not devote himself to a wife and to philosophy at the same time. Cicero does not, indeed,
precisely speak of "devoting himself," but he does
add that he did not wish to undertake anything
which might rival his study of philosophy in its
demands upon him.

Then, turning from the consideration of such
hindrances to the study of philosophy, Heloise
bade me observe what were the conditions of honourable wedlock. What possible concord could
there be between scholars and domestics, between
authors and cradles, between books or tablets and
distaffs, between the stylus or the pen and the
spindle? What man, intent on his religious or philosophical meditations, can possibly endure the
whining of children, the lullabies of the nurse seeking to quiet them, or the noisy confusion of family
life? Who can endure the continual untidiness of

children? The rich, you may reply, can do this, because they have palaces or houses containing many rooms, and because their wealth takes no thought of expense and protects them from daily worries. But to this the answer is that the condition of philosophers is by no means that of the wealthy, nor can those whose minds are occupied with riches and worldly cares find time for religious or philosophical study. For this reason the renowned philosophers of old utterly despised the world, fleeing from its perils rather than reluctantly giving them up, and denied themselves all its delights in order that they might repose in the embraces of philosophy alone. One of them, and the greatest of all, Seneca, in his advice to Lucilius, says philosophy is not a thing to be studied only in hours of leisure; we must give up everything else to devote ourselves to it, for no amount of time is really sufficient hereto" (Epist. 73)

It matters little, she pointed out, whether one abandons the study of philosophy completely or merely interrupts it, for it can never remain at the point where it was thus interrupted. All other occupations must be resisted; it is vain to seek to adjust life to include them, and they must simply be eliminated. This view is maintained, for example, in the love of God by those among us who are truly called monastics, and in the love of wisdom by all those who have stood out among men as sincere philosophers. For in every race, gentiles or Jews or Christians, there have always been a few who excelled their fellows in faith or in the purity of their lives, and who were set apart from the multitude by their continence or by their abstinence from worldly pleasures.

Among the Jews of old there were the Nazarites, who consecrated themselves to the Lord, some of them the sons of the prophet Elias and others the followers of Eliseus, the monks of whom, on the authority of St. Jerome (Epist. 4 and 13), we read in the Old Testament. More recently there were the three philosophical sects which Josephus defines in his Book of Antiquities (xviii. 2), calling them the Pharisees, the Sadducees and the Essenes. In our times, furthermore, there are the monks who imitate either the communal life of the Apostles or the earlier and solitary life of John. Among the gentiles there are, as has been said, the philosophers. Did they not apply the name of wisdom or philosophy as much to the religion of life as to the pursuit of learning, as we find from the origin of the word itself, and likewise from the testimony of the saints?

There is a passage on this subject in the eighth book of St. Augustine's "City of God," wherein he distinguishes between the various schools of philosophy. "The Italian school," he says, "had as its founder Pythagoras of Samos, who, it is said, originated the very word 'philosophy'. Before his time those who were regarded as conspicuous for the praiseworthiness of their lives were called wise men, but he, on being asked of his profession, replied that he was a philosopher, that is to say a student or a lover of wisdom because it seemed to him unduly boastful to call himself a wise man." In this passage, therefore, when the phrase "conspicuous for the praiseworthiness of their lives" is used, it is evident that the wise, in other words the philosophers, were so called less because of their erudition than by reason of their virtuous lives. In what sobriety and continence these men lived it is not for me to prove by illustration, lest I should seem to instruct Minerva herself.

Now, she added, if laymen and gentiles, bound by no profession of religion, lived after this fashion, what ought you, a cleric and a canon, to do in order not to prefer base voluptuousness to your sacred duties, to prevent this Charybdis from sucking you down headlong, and to save yourself from being plunged shamelessly and irrevocably into such filth as this? If you care nothing for your privileges as a cleric, at least uphold your dignity as a philosopher. If you scorn the reverence due to God, let regard for your reputation temper your shamelessness. Remember that Socrates was chained to a wife, and by what a filthy accident he himself paid for this blot on philosophy, in order that others thereafter might be made more cautious by his example. Jerome thus mentions this affair, writing about Socrates in his first book against Jovinianus: "Once when he was withstanding a storm of reproaches which Xantippe was hurling at him from an upper story, he was suddenly drenched with foul slops; wiping his head, he said only, 'I knew there would be a shower after all that thunder.'"

Her final argument was that it would be dangerous for me to take her back to Paris, and that it would be far sweeter for her to be called my mistress than to be known as my wife; nay, too, that this would be more honourable for me as well. In such case, she said, love alone would hold me to her, and the strength of the marriage chain would not constrain us. Even if we should by chance be parted from time to time, the joy of our meetings would be all the sweeter by reason of its rarity. But when she found that she could not convince me or dissuade me from my folly by these and like arguments, and because she could not bear to offend me, with grievous sighs and tears she made an end of her resistance, saying: "Then there is no more left but this, that in our doom the sorrow yet to come shall be no less than the love we two have already known." Nor in this, as now the whole world knows, did she lack the spirit of prophecy.

So, after our little son was born, we left him in my sister's care, and secretly returned to Paris. A few days later, in the early morning, having kept our nocturnal vigil of prayer unknown to all in a certain church, we were united there in the benediction of wedlock her uncle and a few friends of his and mine being present. We departed forthwith stealthily and by separate ways, nor thereafter did we see each other save rarely and in private, thus striving our utmost to conceal what we had done. But her uncle and those of his household, seeking solace for their disgrace, began to divulge the story of our marriage, and thereby to violate the pledge they had given me on this point. Heloise, on the contrary, denounced her own kin and swore that they were speaking the most absolute lies. Her uncle, aroused to fury thereby, visited her repeatedly with punishments. No sooner had I learned this than I sent her to a convent of nuns at Argenteuil, not far from Paris, where she herself had been brought up and educated as a young girl. I had them make ready for her all the garments of a nun, suitable for the life of a convent, excepting only the veil, and these I bade her put on.

When her uncle and his kinsmen heard of this, they were convinced that now I had completely

played them false and had rid myself forever of
Heloise by forcing her to become a nun. Violently
incensed, they laid a plot against me, and one night
while I all unsuspecting was asleep in a secret
room in my lodgings, they broke in with the help of
one of my servants whom they had bribed. There
they had vengeance on me with a most cruel and
most shameful punishment, such as astounded the
whole world; for they cut off those parts of my
body with which I had done that which was the
cause of their sorrow. This done, straightway they
fled, but two of them were captured and suffered
the loss of their eyes and their genital organs. One
of these two was the aforesaid servant, who even
while he was still in my service, had been led by his
avarice to betray me.

Chapter Eight - Of the Suffering of His Body

OF HOW HE BECAME A MONK IN THE MONASTERY OF ST. DENIS AND HELOISE A NUN AT ARGENTEUIL

WHEN morning came the whole city was assembled before my dwelling. It is difficult, nay, impossible, for words of mine to describe the amazement which bewildered them, the lamentations they uttered, the uproar with which they harassed me, or the grief with which they increased my own suffering. Chiefly the clerics, and above all my scholars, tortured me with their intolerable lamentations and outcries, so that I suffered more intensely from their compassion than from the pain of my wound. In truth I felt the disgrace more than the hurt to my body, and was more afflicted with shame than with pain. My incessant thought was of the renown in which I had so much delighted, now brought low, nay, utterly blotted out, so swiftly by an evil chance. I saw, too, how justly God had punished me in that very part of my body whereby I had sinned. I perceived that there was indeed justice in my betrayal by him whom I had myself already betrayed; and then I thought how eagerly my rivals would seize upon this manifestation of justice, how this disgrace would bring bitter and enduring grief to my kindred and my friends, and how the tale of this amazing outrage would spread to the very ends of the earth.

What path lay open to me thereafter? How could I ever again hold up my head among men, when every finger should be pointed at me in scorn, every tongue speak my blistering shame, and when I should be a monstrous spectacle to all eyes? I was overwhelmed by the remembrance that, according to the dread letter of the law, God holds eunuchs in such abomination that men thus maimed are forbidden to enter a church, even as the unclean and filthy; nay, even beasts in such plight were not acceptable as sacrifices. Thus in Leviticus (xxii. 24) is it said: "Ye shall not offer unto the Lord that which hath its stones bruised, or crushed, or broken, or cut." And in Deuteronomy (xxiii. 1), "He that is wounded in the stones, or hath his privy member cut off, shall not enter into the congregation of the Lord."

I must confess that in my misery it was the overwhelming sense of my disgrace rather than any ardour for conversion to the religious life that drove me to seek the seclusion of the monastic cloister. Heloise had already, at my bidding, taken the veil and entered a convent. Thus it was that we both put on the sacred garb, I in the abbey of St. Denis, and she in the convent of Argenteuil, of which I have already spoken. She, I remember well, when her fond friends sought vainly to deter her from submitting her fresh youth to the heavy and almost intolerable yoke of monastic life, sobbing and weeping replied in the words of Cornelia:

"O husband most noble
Who ne'er shouldst have shared my couch! Has fortune such power
To smite so lofty a head? Why then was I wedded
Only to bring thee to woe? Receive now my sorrow,
The price I so gladly pay."
- (Lucan, "Pharsalia," viii. 94.)

With these words on her lips did she go forthwith to the altar, and lifted therefrom the veil, which had been blessed by the bishop, and before them all she took the vows of the religious life. For my part, scarcely had I recovered from my wound when clerics sought me in great numbers, endlessly beseeching both my abbot and me myself that now, since I was done with learning for the sake of pain or renown, I should turn to it for the sole love of God. They bade me care diligently for the talent which God had committed to my keeping (Matthew, xxv. 15), since surely He would demand it back from me with interest. It was their plea that, inasmuch as of old I had laboured chiefly in behalf of the rich, I should now devote myself to the teaching of the poor. Therein above all should I perceive how it was the hand of God that had touched me, when I should devote my life to the study of letters in freedom from the snares of the flesh and withdrawn from the tumultuous life of this world. Thus, in truth, should I become a philosopher less of this world than of God.

The abbey, however, to which I had betaken myself was utterly worldly and in its life quite scandalous. The abbot himself was as far below his fellows in his way of living and in the foulness of his reputation as he was above them in priestly rank. This intolerable state of things I often and vehemently denounced, sometimes in private talk and sometimes publicly, but the only result was that I made myself detested of them all. They gladly laid hold of the daily eagerness of my students to hear me as an excuse whereby they might be rid of me; and finally, at the insistent urging of the students themselves, and with the hearty consent of the abbot and the rest of the brotherhood, I departed thence to a certain hut, there to teach in my wonted way. To this place such a throng of students flocked that the neighbourhood could not afford shelter for them, nor the earth sufficient sustenance.

Here, as befitted my profession, I devoted myself chiefly to lectures on theology, but I did not wholly abandon the teaching of the secular arts, to which I was more accustomed, and which was particularly demanded of me. I used the latter, however, as a hook, luring my students by the bait of learning to the study of the true philosophy, even as the Ecclesiastical History tells of Origen, the greatest of all Christian philosophers. Since apparently the Lord had gifted me with no less persuasiveness in expounding the Scriptures than in lecturing on secular subjects, the number of my students in these two courses began to increase greatly, and the attendance at all the other schools was correspondingly diminished. Thus I aroused the envy and hatred of the other teachers. Those way took who sought to belittle me in every possible advantage of my absence to bring two principal charges against me: first, that it was contrary to the monastic profession to be concerned with the study of secular books; and, second, that I had presumed to teach theology without ever having been taught therein myself. This they did in order that my teaching of every kind might be prohibited, and to this end they continually stirred up bishops, archbishops, abbots and whatever other dignitaries of the Church they could reach.

Chapter Nine - Of His Book on Theology and His Persecution at The Hands of His Fellow Students of The Council Against Him

IT SO happened that at the outset I devoted myself to analysing the basis of our faith through illustrations based on human understanding, and I wrote for my students a certain tract on the unity and trinity of God. This I did because they were always seeking for rational and philosophical explanations, asking rather for reasons they could understand than for mere words, saying that it was futile to utter words which the intellect could not possibly follow, that nothing could be believed unless it could first be understood, and that it was absurd for any one to preach to others a thing which neither he himself nor those whom he sought to teach could comprehend. Our Lord Himself maintained this same thing when He said: "They are blind leaders of the blind" (Matthew, xv. 14).

Now, a great many people saw and read this tract, and it became exceedingly popular, its clearness appealing particularly to all who sought information on this subject. And since the questions involved are generally considered the most difficult of all, their complexity is taken as the measure of the subtlety of him who succeeds in answering them. As a result, my rivals became furiously angry, and summoned a council to take action against me, the chief instigators therein being my two intriguing enemies of former days, Alberic and Lotulphe. These two, now that both William and Anselm, our erstwhile teachers, we're dead, were greedy to reign in their stead, and, so to speak, to succeed them as heirs. While they were directing the school at Rheims, they managed by repeated hints to stir up their archbishop, Rodolphe, against me, for the purpose of holding a meeting, or rather an ecclesiastical council, at Soissons, provided they could secure the approval of Conon, Bishop of Praeneste, at that time papal legate in France. Their plan was to summon me to be present at this council, bringing with me the famous book I had written regarding the Trinity. In all this, indeed, they were successful, and the thing happened according to their wishes.

Before I reached Soissons, however, these two rivals of mine so foully slandered me with both the clergy and the public that on the day of my arrival the people came near to stoning me and the few students of mine who had accompanied me thither. The cause of their anger was that they had been led to believe that I had preached and written to prove the existence of three gods. No sooner had I reached the city, therefore, than I went forthwith to the legate; to him I submitted my book for examination and judgment, declaring that if I had written anything repugnant to the Catholic faith, I was quite ready to correct it or otherwise to make satisfactory amends. The legate directed me to refer my book to the archbishop and to those same two rivals of mine, to the end that my accusers might also be my judges. So in my case was fulfilled the saying: "Even our enemies are our judges" (Deut. xxxii. 31).

These three, then, took my book and pawed it over and examined it minutely, but could find nothing therein which they dared to use as the basis for a public accusation against me. Accordingly they put off the condemnation of the book until the close of the council, despite their eagerness to bring it about. For my part, every day before the council convened I publicly discussed the Catholic faith in the light of what I had written, and all who heard me were enthusiastic in their approval alike of the frankness and the logic of my words. When the public and the clergy had thus learned something of the real character of my teaching, they began to say to one another: "Behold, now he speaks openly, and no one brings any charge against him. And this council, summoned, as we have heard, chiefly to take action upon his case is drawing toward its end. Did the judges realize that the error might be theirs rather than his?"

As a result of all this, my rivals grew more angry day by day. On one occasion Alberic, accompanied by some of his students, came to me for the purpose of intimidating me, and, after a few bland words, said that he was amazed at something he had found in my book, to the effect that, although God had begotten God, I denied that God had begotten Himself, since there was only one God. I answered unhesitatingly: "I can give you an explanation of this if you wish it." "Nay," he replied, "I care nothing for human explanation or reasoning in such matters, but only for the words of authority." "Very well, I said; "turn the pages of my book and you will find the authority likewise." The book was at hand, for he had brought it with him. I turned to the passage I had in mind, which he had either not discovered or else passed over as containing nothing injurious to me. And it was God's will that I quickly found what I sought. This was the following sentence, under the heading "Augustine, On the

Trinity, Book I": "Whosoever believes that it is within the power of God to beget Himself is sorely in error; this power is not in God, neither is it in any created thing, spiritual or corporeal. For there is nothing that can give birth to itself."

When those of his followers who were present heard this, they were amazed and much embarrassed. He himself, in order to keep his countenance, said: "Certainly, I understand all that." Then I added: "What I have to say further on this subject is by no means new, but apparently it has nothing to do with the case at issue, since you have asked for the word of authority only, and not for explanations. If, however, you care to consider logical explanations, I am prepared to demonstrate that, according to Augustine's statement, you have yourself fallen into a heresy in believing that a father can possibly be his own son." When Alberic heard this he was almost beside himself with rage, and straightway resorted to threats, asserting that neither my explanations nor my citations of authority would avail me aught in this case. With this he left me.

On the last day of the council, before the session convened, the legate and the archbishop deliberated with my rivals and sundry others as to what should be. done about me and my book, this being the chief reason for their having come together.

And since they had discovered nothing either in my speech or in what I had hitherto written which would give them a case against me, they were all reduced to silence, or at the most to maligning me in whispers. Then Geoffroi, Bishop of Chartres, who excelled the other bishops alike in the sincerity of his religion and in the importance of his see, spoke thus:

"You know, my lords, all who are gathered here, the doctrine of this man, what it is, and his ability, which has brought him many followers in every field to which he has devoted himself. You know how greatly he has lessened the renown of other teachers, both his masters and our own, and how he has spread as it were the offshoots of his vine from sea to sea. Now, if you impose a lightly considered judgment on him, as I cannot believe you will, you well know that even if mayhap you are in the right there are many who will be angered thereby and that he will have no lack of defenders. Remember above all that we have found nothing in this book of his that lies before us whereon any open accusation can be based. Indeed it is true, as Jerome says: `Fortitude openly displayed always creates rivals, and the lightning strikes the highest peaks.' Have a care, then, lest by violent action you only increase his fame, and lest we do more hurt to ourselves through envy than to him through justice. A false report, as that same wise man reminds us, is easily crushed, and a man's later life gives testimony as to his earlier deeds. If, then, you are disposed to take canonical action against him, his doctrine or his writings must be brought forward as evidence, and he must have free opportunity to answer his questioners. In that case if he is found guilty or if he confesses his error, his lips can be wholly sealed. Consider the words of the blessed Nicodemus, who, desiring to free Our Lord Himself, said: 'Doth our law judge any man before it hear him and know what he doeth? (John, vii. 51).

When my rivals heard this they cried out in protest, saying: "This is wise counsel, forsooth, that we should strive against the wordiness of this man, whose arguments, or rather, sophistries, the whole world cannot resist!" And yet, methinks, it was far more difficult to strive against Christ Himself, for Whom, nevertheless, Nicodemus demanded a hearing in accordance with the dictates of the law. When the bishop could not win their assent to his proposals, he tried in another way to curb their hatred, saying that for the discussion of such an important case the few who were present were not enough, and that this matter required a more thorough examination. His further suggestion was that my abbot, who was there present, should take me back with him to our abbey, in other words to the monastery of St. Denis, and that there a large convocation of learned men should determine, on the basis of a careful investigation, what ought to be done. To this last proposal the legate consented, as did all the others.

Then the legate arose to celebrate mass before entering the council, and through the bishop sent me the permission which had been determined on, authorizing me to return to my monastery and there await such action as might be finally taken. But my rivals, perceiving that they would accomplish nothing if the trial were to be held outside of their own diocese, and in a place where they could have little influence on the verdict, and in truth having small wish that justice should be done, persuaded the archbishop that it would be a grave insult to him to transfer this case to another court, and that it would be dangerous for him if by chance I should thus be acquitted. They likewise went to the legate, and succeeded in so changing his opinion that finally they induced him to frame a new sentence, whereby he agreed to condemn my book without any further inquiry, to burn it forthwith in the sight of all, and to confine me for a year in another monastery. The argument they used was that it sufficed for the condemnation of my book that I had presumed to read it in public without the approval either of the Roman pontiff or of the church, and that, furthermore, I had given it to many to be transcribed. Methinks it would be a notable blessing to the Christian faith if there were more who displayed a like presumption. The legate, however, being less skilled in law than he should have been, relied chiefly on the advice of the archbishop, and he, in turn, on that of my rivals. When the Bishop of Chartres got wind of this, he reported the whole conspiracy to me, and strongly urged me to endure meekly the manifest violence of their enmity. He bade me not to doubt that this violence would in the end react upon them and prove a blessing to me, and counseled me to have no fear of the confinement in a monastery, knowing that within a few days the legate himself, who was now acting under compulsion, would after his departure set me free. And thus he consoled me as best he might, mingling his tears with mine.

Chapter Ten - Of the Burning of His Book

OF THE PERSECUTION HE HAD AT THE HANDS OF HIS ABBOT AND THE BRETHREN

STRAIGHTWAY upon my summons I went to the council, and there, without further examination or debate, did they compel me with my own hand to cast that memorable book of mine into the flames. Although my enemies appeared to have nothing to say while the book was burning, one of them muttered something about having seen it written therein that God the Father was alone omnipotent. This reached the ears of the legate, who replied in astonishment that he could not believe that even a child would make so absurd a blunder. "Our common faith," he said, holds and sets forth that the Three are alike omnipotent." A certain Tirric, a schoolmaster, hearing this, sarcastically added the Athanasian phrase, "And yet there are not three omnipotent Persons, but only One."

This man's bishop forthwith began to censure him, bidding him desist from such treasonable talk, but he boldly stood his ground, and said, as if quoting the words of Daniel: " 'Are ye such fools, ye sons of Israel, that without examination or knowledge of the truth ye have condemned a daughter of Israel? Return again to the place of judgment,' (Daniel, xiii. 48 The History of Susanna) and there give judgment on the judge himself. You have set up this judge, forsooth, for the instruction of faith and the correction of error, and yet, when he ought to give judgment, he condemns himself out of his own mouth. Set free today, with the help of God's mercy, one who is manifestly innocent, even as Susanna was freed of old from her false accusers."

Thereupon the archbishop arose and confirmed the legate's statement, but changed the wording thereof, as indeed was most fitting. "It is God's truth," he said, "that the Father is omnipotent, the Son is omnipotent, the Holy Spirit is omnipotent. And whosoever dissents from this is openly in error, and must not be listened to. Nevertheless, if it be your pleasure, it would be well that this our brother should publicly state before us all the faith that is in him, to the end that, according to its deserts, it may either be approved or else condemned and corrected."

When, however, I fain would have arisen to pro-
fess and set forth my faith, in order that I might
express in my own words that which was in my
heart, my enemies declared that it was not needful
for me to do more than recite the Athanasian Sym-
bol, a thing which any boy might do as well as I.
And lest I should allege ignorance, pretending that
I did not know the words by heart, they had a copy
of it set before me to read. And read it I did as best
I could for my groans and sighs and tears. Thereupon, as if I had been a convicted criminal, I was
handed over to the Abbot of St. Médard, who was
there present, and led to his monastery as to a
prison. And with this the council was immediately
dissolved.

The abbot and the monks of the aforesaid monastery, thinking that I would remain long with
them, received me with great exultation, and diligently sought to console me, but all in vain. O God,
who dost judge justice itself, in what venom of the
spirit, in what bitterness of mind, did I blame even
Thee for my shame, accusing Thee in my madness!
Full often did I repeat the lament of St. Anthony:
"Kindly Jesus, where wert Thou?" The sorrow that
tortured me, the shame that overwhelmed me, the
desperation that wracked my mind, all these I
could then feel, but even now I can find no words
to express them. Comparing these new sufferings

of my soul with those I had formerly endured in my body, it seemed that I was in very truth the most miserable among men. Indeed that earlier betrayal had become a little thing in comparison with this later evil, and I lamented the hurt to my fair name far more than the one to my body. The latter, indeed, I had brought upon myself through my own wrongdoing, but this other violence had come upon me solely by reason of the honesty of my purpose and my love of our faith, which had compelled me to write that which I believed.

The very cruelty and heartlessness of my punishment, however, made every one who heard the story vehement in censuring it, so that those who had a hand therein were soon eager to disclaim all responsibility, shouldering the blame on others. Nay, matters came to such a pass that even my rivals denied that they had had anything to do with the matter, and as for the legate, he publicly denounced the malice with which the French had acted. Swayed by repentance for his injustice, and feeling that he had yielded enough to satisfy their rancour he shortly freed me from the monastery whither I had been taken, and sent me back to my own. Here, however, I found almost as many enemies as I had in the former days of which I have already spoken, for the vileness and shamelessness of their way of living made them realize that they would again have to endure my censure.

After a few months had passed, chance gave them an opportunity by which they sought to destroy me. It happened that one day, in the course of my reading, I came upon a certain passage of Bede, in his commentary on the Acts of the Apostles, wherein he asserts that Dionysius the Areopagite was the bishop, not of Athens, but of Corinth. Now, this was directly counter to the belief of the monks, who were wont to boast that their Dionysius, or Denis, was not only the Areopagite but was likewise proved by his acts to have been the Bishop of Athens. Having thus found this testimony of Bede's in contradiction of our own tradition, I showed it somewhat jestingly to sundry of the monks who chanced to be near. Wrathfully they declared that Bede was no better than a liar, and that they had a far more trustworthy authority in the person of Hilduin, a former abbot of theirs, who had travelled for a long time throughout Greece for the purpose of investigating this very question. He, they insisted, had by his writings removed all possible doubt on the subject, and had securely established the truth of the traditional belief.

One of the monks went so far as to ask me brazenly which of the two, Bede or Hilduin, I considered the better authority on this point. I replied that the authority of Bede, whose writings are held in high esteem by the whole Latin Church, appeared to me the better. Thereupon in a great rage they began to cry out that at last I had openly proved the hatred I had always felt for our monastery, and that I was seeking to disgrace it in the eyes of the whole kingdom, robbing it of the honour in which it had particularly gloried, by thus denying that the Areopagite was their patron saint. To this I answered that I had never denied the fact, and that I did not much care whether their patron was the Areopagite or some one else, provided only he had received his crown from God. Thereupon they ran to the abbot and told him of the misdemeanour with which they charged me.

The abbot listened to their story with delight, rejoicing at having found a chance to crush me, for the greater vileness of his life made him fear me more even than the rest did. Accordingly he summoned his council, and when the brethren had assembled he violently threatened me, declaring that he would straightway send me to the king, by him to be punished for having thus sullied his crown and the glory of his royalty. And until he should hand me over to the king, he ordered that I should be closely guarded. In vain did I offer to submit to the customary discipline if I had in any way been guilty. Then, horrified at their wickedness, which

seemed to crown the ill fortune I had so long endured, and in utter despair at the apparent conspiracy of the whole world against me, I fled secretly from the monastery by night, helped thereto
by some of the monks who took pity on me, and
likewise aided by some of my scholars.

I made my way to a region where I had formerly
dwelt, hard by the lands of Count Theobald (of
Champagne). He himself had some slight acquaint-
ance with me, and had compassion on me by reason of my persecutions, of which the story had
reached him. I found a home there within the walls
of Provins, in a priory of the monks of Troyes, the
prior of which had in former days known me well
and shown me much love. In his joy at my coming
he cared for me with all diligence. It chanced, however, that one day my abbot came to Provins to see
the count on certain matters of business. As soon
as I had learned of this, I went to the count, the
prior accompanying me, and besought him to in-
tercede in my behalf with the abbot. I asked no
more than that the abbot should absolve me of the
charge against me, and give me permission to live
the monastic life wheresoever I could find a suitable place. The abbot, however, and those who were
with him took the matter under advisement, saying
that they would give the count an answer the day
before they departed. It appeared from their words

that they thought I wished to go to some other abbey, a thing which they regarded as an immense disgrace to their own. They had, indeed, taken particular pride in the fact that, upon my conversion, I had come to them, as if scorning all other abbeys, and accordingly they considered that it would bring great shame upon them if I should now desert their abbey and seek another. For this reason they refused to listen either to my own plea or to that of the count. Furthermore, they threatened me with excommunication unless I should instantly return; likewise they forbade the prior with whom I had taken refuge to keep me longer, under pain of sharing my excommunication. When we heard this both the prior and I were stricken with fear. The abbot went away still obdurate, but a few days thereafter he died.

As soon as his successor had been named, I went to him, accompanied by the Bishop of Meaux, to try if I might win from him the permission I had vainly sought of his predecessor. At first he would not give his assent, but finally, through the intervention of certain friends of mine, I secured the right to appeal to the king and his council, and in this way I at last obtained what I sought. The royal seneschal, Stephen, having summoned the abbot and his subordinates that they might state their case, asked them why they wanted to keep me against my will. He pointed out that this might easily bring them into evil repute, and certainly could do them no good, seeing that their way of living was utterly incompatible with mine. I knew it to be the opinion of the royal council that the irregularities in the conduct of this abbey would tend to bring it more and more under the control of the king, making it increasingly useful and likewise profitable to him, and for this reason I had good hope of easily winning the support of the king and those about him.

Thus, indeed, did it come to pass. But in order that the monastery might not be shorn of any of the glory which it had enjoyed by reason of my sojourn there, they granted me permission to betake myself to any solitary place I might choose, provided only I did not put myself under the rule of any other abbey. This was agreed upon and confirmed on both sides in the presence of the king and his councellors. Forthwith I sought out a lonely spot known to me of old in the region of Troyes, and there, on a bit of land which had been given to me, and with the approval of the bishop of the district, I built with reeds and stalks my first oratory in the name of the Holy Trinity. And there concealed, with but one comrade, a certain cleric, I was able to sing over and over again to the Lord: "Lo, then would I wander far off, and remain in the wilderness" (Ps. iv. 7).

Chapter Eleven - Of His Teaching in the Wilderness

NO SOONER had scholars learned of my retreat than they began to flock thither from all sides, leaving their towns and castles to dwell in the wilderness. In place of their spacious houses they built themselves huts; instead of dainty fare they lived on the herbs of the field and coarse bread; their soft beds they exchanged for heaps of straw and rushes, and their tables were piles of turf. in very truth you may well believe that they were like those philosophers of old of whom Jerome tells us in his second book against Jovinianus.

"Through the senses," says Jerome, "as through so many windows, do vices win entrance to the soul. The metropolis and citadel of the mind cannot be taken unless the army of the foe has first rushed in through the gates. If any one delights in the games of the circus, in the contests of athletes, in the versatility of actors, in the beauty of women, in the glitter of gems and raiment, or in aught else like to these, then the freedom of his soul is made captive through the windows of his eyes, and thus is fulfilled the prophecy: 'For death is come up into our windows' (Jer. ix. 21). And then, when the wedges of doubt have, as it were, been driven into the citadels of our minds through these gateways, where will be its liberty? where its fortitude? where its thought of God? Most of all does the sense of touch paint for itself the pictures of past raptures, compelling the soul to dwell fondly upon remembered iniquities, and so to practice in imagination those things which reality denies to it.

"Heeding such counsel, therefore, many among the philosophers forsook the thronging ways of the cities and the pleasant gardens of the countryside, with their well watered fields, their shady trees, the song of birds, the mirror of the fountain, the murmur of the stream, the many charms for eye and ear, fearing lest their souls should grow soft amid luxury and abundance of riches, and lest their virtue should thereby be defiled. For it is perilous to turn your eyes often to those things whereby you may some day be made captive, or to attempt the possession of that which it would go hard with you to do without. Thus the Pythagoreans shunned all companionship of this kind, and were wont to dwell in solitary and desert places. Nay, Plato himself, although he was a rich man let Diogenes trample on his couch with muddy feet, and in order that he might devote himself to philosophy established his academy in a place remote from the city, and not only uninhabited but unhealthy as well. This he did in order that the onslaughts of lust might be broken by the fear and constant presence of disease, and that his followers might find no pleasure save in the things they learned."

————— Such a life, likewise, the sons of the prophets who were the followers of Eliseus are reported to have led. Of these Jerome also tells us, writing thus to the monk Rusticus as if describing the monks of those ancient days: "The sons of the prophets, the monks of whom we read in the Old Testament built for themselves huts by the waters of the Jordan, and forsaking the throngs and the cities, lived on pottage and the herbs of the field" (Epist. iv).

Even so did my followers build their huts above the waters of the Arduzon, so that they seemed hermits rather than scholars. And as their number grew ever greater, the hardships which they gladly endured for the sake of my teaching seemed to my rivals to reflect new glory on me, and to cast new shame on themselves. Nor was it strange that they, who had done their utmost to hurt me, should grieve to see how all things worked together for my good, even though I was now, in the words of Jerome, afar from cities and the market place, from controversies and the crowded ways of men. And so, as Quintilian says, did envy seek me out even in my hiding place. Secretly my rivals complained and lamented one to another, saying: "Behold now, the whole world runs after him, and our persecution of him has done nought save to increase his glory. We strove to extinguish his fame, and we have but given it new brightness. Lo, in the cities scholars have at hand everything they may need, and yet, spurning the pleasures of the town, they seek out the barrenness of the desert, and of their own free will they accept wretchedness."

The thing which at that time chiefly led me to undertake the direction of a school was my intolerable poverty, for I had not strength enough to dig, and shame kept me from begging. And so, resorting once more to the art with which I was so familiar, I was compelled to substitute the service of the tongue for the labour of my hands. The students willingly provided me with whatsoever I needed in the way of food and clothing, and likewise took charge of the cultivation of the fields and paid for the erection of buildings, in order that material cares might not keep me from my studies. Since my oratory was no longer large enough to hold even a small part of their number, they found it necessary to increase its size, and in so doing they greatly improved it, building it of stone and wood. Although this oratory had been founded in

honour of the Holy Trinity, and afterwards dedicated thereto, I now named it the Paraclete, mind-
ful of how I had come there a fugitive and in despair, and had breathed into my soul something of
the miracle of divine consolation.

Many of those who heard of this were greatly
astonished, and some violently assailed my action,
declaring that it was not permissible to dedicate a
church exclusively to the Holy Spirit rather than to
God the Father. They held, according to an ancient
tradition, that 'it must be dedicated either to the
Son alone or else to the entire Trinity. The error
which led them into this false accusation resulted
from their failure to perceive the identity of the
Paraclete with the Spirit Paraclete. Even as the
whole Trinity, or any Person in the Trinity, may
rightly be called God or Helper, so likewise may It
be termed the Paraclete, that is to say the Consoler.
These are the words of the Apostle: "Blessed be
God, even the Father of our Lord Jesus Christ, the
Father of mercies, and the God of all comfort; who
comforteth us in all our tribulation" (II Cor. i. 3)
And likewise the word of truth says: "And he shall
give you another comforter" (Greek "another Paraclete," John, xiv. 16).

Nay, since every church is consecrated equally in
the name of the Father, the Son and the Holy Spirit,
without any difference in their possession thereof,

why should not the house of God be dedicated to the Father or to the Holy Spirit, even as it is to the Son? Who would presume to erase from above the door the name of him who is the master of the house? And since the Son offered Himself as a sacrifice to the Father, and accordingly in the ceremonies of the mass the prayers are offered particularly to the Father, and the immolation of the Host is made to Him, why should the altar not be held to be chiefly His to whom above all the supplication and sacrifice are made? Is it not called more rightly the altar of Him who receives than of Him who makes the sacrifice? Who would admit that an altar is that of the Holy Cross, or of the Sepulchre, or of St. Michael, or John, or Peter, or of any other saint, unless either he himself was sacrificed there or else special sacrifices and prayers are made there to him? Methinks the altars and temples of certain ones among these saints are not held to be idolatrous even though they are used for special sacrifices and prayers to their patrons.

Some, however, may perchance argue that churches are not built or altars dedicated to the Father because there is no feast which is solemnized especially for Him. But while this reasoning holds good as regards the Trinity itself, it does not apply in the case of the Holy Spirit. For this Spirit, from the day of Its advent, has had its special feast of the

Pentecost, even as the Son has had since His coming upon earth His feast of the Nativity. Even as the Son was sent into this world, so did the Holy Spirit descend upon the disciples, and thus does It claim Its special religious rites. Nay, it seems more fitting to dedicate a temple to It than to either of the other Persons of the Trinity, if we but carefully study the apostolic authority, and consider the workings of this Spirit Itself. To none of the three Persons did the apostle dedicate a special temple save to the Holy Spirit alone. He does not speak of a temple of the Father, or a temple of the Son, as he does of a temple of the Holy Spirit, writing thus in his first epistle to the Corinthians: "But he that is joined unto the Lord is one spirit." (I Cor. vi. 17). And again: "What? know ye not that your body is the temple of the Holy Spirit which is in you, which ye have of God, and ye are not your own?" (ib. 19).

Who is there who does not know that the sacraments of God's blessings pertaining to the Church are particularly ascribed to the operation of divine grace, by which is meant the Holy Spirit? Forsooth we are born again of water and of the Holy Spirit in baptism, and thus from the very beginning is the body made, as it were, a special temple of God. In the successive sacraments, moreover, the sevenfold grace of the Spirit is added, whereby this same temple of God is made beautiful and is consecrated.

What wonder is it, then, if to that Person to Whom the apostle assigned a spiritual temple we should dedicate a material one? Or to what Person can a church be more rightly said to belong than to Him to Whom all the blessings which the church administers are particularly ascribed? It was not, however, with the thought of dedicating my oratory to one Person that I first called it the Paraclete, but for the reason I have already told, that in this spot I found consolation. None the less, even if I had done it for the reason attributed to me, the departure from the usual custom would have been in no way illogical.

Chapter Twelve - Of the Persecution Directed Against Him by Sundry New Enemies Or, As It Were, Apostles

A<small>ND</small> so I dwelt in this place, my body indeed hidden away, but my fame spreading throughout the whole world, till its echo reverberated mightily—echo, that fancy of the poet's, which has so great a voice, and nought beside. My former rivals, seeing that they themselves were now powerless to do me hurt, stirred up against me certain new apostles in whom the world put great faith. One of these (Norbert of Prémontré) took pride in his position as canon of a regular order; the other (Bernard of Clairvaux) made it his boast that he bad revived the true monastic life. These two ran hither and yon preaching and shamelessly slandering me in every way they could, so that in time they succeeded in drawing down on my head the scorn of many among those having authority, among both the clergy and the laity. They spread abroad such sinister reports of my faith as well as of my life that they turned even my best friends against me, and those who still retained something of their former regard for me were fain to disguise it in every possible way by reason of their fear of these two men.

God is my witness that whensoever I learned of the convening of a new assemblage of the clergy, I believed that it was done for the express purpose of my condemnation. Stunned by this fear like one smitten with a thunderbolt, I daily expected to be dragged before their councils or assemblies as a heretic or one guilty of impiety. Though I seem to compare a flea with a lion, or an ant with an elephant, in very truth my rivals persecuted me no less bitterly than the heretics of old hounded St. Athanasius. Often, God knows, I sank so deep in despair that I was ready to leave the world of Christendom and go forth among the heathen, paying them a stipulated tribute in order that I might live quietly a Christian life among the enemies of Christ. It seemed to me that such people might indeed be kindly disposed toward me, particularly as they would doubtless suspect me of being no good Christian, imputing my flight to some crime I had committed, and would therefore believe that I might perhaps be won over to their form of worship.

Chapter Thirteen - Of the Abbey to Which He Was Called

...and of the Persecution He Had from His Sons That Is to Say the Monks and From the Lord of the Land

WHILE I was thus afflicted with so great perturbation to of the spirit, and when the only way of escape seemed to be for me to seek refuge with Christ among the enemies of Christ, there came a chance whereby I thought I could for a while avoid the plottings of my enemies. But thereby I fell among Christians and monks who were far more savage than heathens and more evil of life. The thing came about in this wise. There was in lesser Brittany, in the bishopric of Vannes, a certain abbey of St. Gildas at Ruits, then mourning the death of its shepherd. To this abbey the elective choice of the brethren called me, with the approval of the prince of that land, and I easily secured permission to accept the post from my own abbot and brethren. Thus did the hatred of the French drive me westward, even as that of the Romans drove Jerome toward the East. Never, God knows, would I have agreed to this thing had it not been for my longing for any possible means of escape from the sufferings which I had borne so constantly.

The land was barbarous and its speech was unknown to me; as for the monks, their vile and untameable way of life was notorious almost everywhere. The people of the region, too, were uncivilized and lawless. Thus, like one who in terror of the sword that threatens him dashes headlong over a precipice, and to shun one death for a moment rushes to another, I knowingly sought this new danger in order to escape from the former one. And there, amid the dreadful roar of the waves of the sea, where the land's end left me no further refuge in flight, often in my prayers did I repeat over and over again: "From the end of the earth will I cry unto Thee, when my heart is overwhelmed" (Ps. lxi. 2).

No one, methinks, could fail to understand how persistently that undisciplined body of monks, the direction of which I had thus undertaken, tortured my heart day and night, or how constantly I was compelled to think of the danger alike to my body and to my soul. I held it for certain that if I should try to force them to live according to the principles they had themselves professed, I should not survive. And yet, if I did not do this to the utmost of my ability, I saw that my damnation was assured. Moreover, a certain lord who was exceedingly powerful in that region had some time previously brought the abbey under his control, taking advantage of the state of disorder within the monastery to seize all the lands adjacent thereto for his own use, and he ground down the monks with taxes heavier than those which were extorted from the Jews themselves.

The monks pressed me to supply them with their daily necessities, but they held no property in common which I might administer in their behalf, and each one, with such resources as he possessed, supported himself and his concubines, as well as his sons and daughters. They took delight in harassing me on this matter, and they stole and carried off whatsoever they could lay their hands on, to the end that my failure to maintain order might make me either give up trying to enforce discipline or else abandon my post altogether. Since the entire region was equally savage, lawless and disorganized, there was not a single man to whom I could turn for aid, for the habits of all alike were foreign to me. Outside the monastery the lord and his henchmen ceaselessly hounded me, and within its walls the brethren were forever plotting against me, so that it seemed as if the Apostle had had me and none other in mind when he I said: "Without were fightings, within were fears" (II Cor. vii. 5).

I considered and lamented the uselessness and the wretchedness of my existence, how fruitless my life now was, both to myself and to others; how of old I had been of some service to the clerics whom I had now abandoned for the sake of these monks, so that I was no longer able to be of use to either; how incapable I had proved myself in everything I had undertaken or attempted, so that above all others I deserved the reproach, "This man began to build, and was not able to finish" (Luke xiv. 30). My despair grew still deeper when I compared the evils I had left behind with those to which I had come, for my former sufferings now seemed to me as nought. Full often did I groan: "Justly has this sorrow come upon me because I deserted the Paraclete, which is to say the Consoler, and thrust myself into sure desolation; seeking to shun threats I fled to certain peril."

The thing which tormented me most was the fact that, having abandoned my oratory, I could make no suitable provision for the celebration there of the divine office, for indeed the extreme poverty of the place would scarcely provide the necessities of one man. But the true Paraclete Himself brought me real consolation in the midst of this sorrow of mine, and made all due provision for His own oratory. For it chanced that in some manner or other, laying claim to it as having legally belonged in earlier days to his monastery, my abbot of St. Denis got possession of the abbey of Argenteuil, of which I have previously spoken, wherein she who was now my sister in Christ rather than my wife, Heloise, had taken the veil. From this abbey he expelled by force all the nuns who had dwelt there, and of whom my former companion had become the prioress. The exiles being thus dispersed in various places, I perceived that this was an opportunity presented by God himself to me whereby I could make provision anew for my oratory. And so, returning thither, I bade her come to the oratory, together with some others from the same convent who had clung to her.

On their arrival there I made over to them the oratory, together with everything pertaining thereto, and subsequently, through the approval and assistance of the bishop of the district, Pope Innocent II promulgated a decree confirming my gift in perpetuity to them and their successors. And this refuge of divine mercy, which they served so devotedly, soon brought them consolation, even though at first their life there was one of want, and for a time of utter destitution. But the place proved itself a true Paraclete to them, making all those who dwelt

round about feel pity and kindliness for the sister-
hood. So that, methinks, they prospered more
through gifts in a single year than I should have
done if I had stayed there a hundred. True it is that
the weakness of womankind makes their needs
and sufferings appeal strongly to people's feelings,
as likewise it makes their virtue all the more pleasing to God and man. And God granted such favour
in the eyes of all to her who was now my sister,
and who was in authority over the rest, that the
bishops loved her as a daughter, the abbots as a
sister, and the laity as a mother. All alike marvelled
at her religious zeal, her good judgment and the
sweetness of her incomparable patience in all
things. The less often she allowed herself to be
seen, shutting herself up in her cell to devote herself to sacred meditations and prayers, the more
eagerly did those who dwelt without demand her
presence and the spiritual guidance of her words.

Chapter Fourteen - Of the Vile Report of His Iniquity

BEFORE long all those who dwelt thereabouts began to censure me roundly, complaining that I paid far less attention to their needs than I might and should have done, and that at least I could do something for them through my preaching. As a result, I returned thither frequently, to be of service to them in whatsoever way I could. Regarding this there was no lack of hateful murmuring, and the thing which sincere charity induced me to do was seized upon by the wickedness of my detractors as the subject of shameless outcry. They declared that I, who of old could scarcely endure to be parted from her I loved, was still swayed by the delights of fleshly lust. Many times I thought of the complaint of St. Jerome in his letter to Asella regarding those women whom he was falsely accused of loving when he said (Epist. xcix): "I am charged with nothing save the fact of my sex, and this charge is made only because Paula is setting forth to Jerusalem." And again: "Before I became intimate in the household of the saintly Paula, the whole city was loud in my praise, and nearly every one deemed me deserving of the highest honours of priesthood. But I know that my way to the kingdom of Heaven lies through good and evil report alike."

When I pondered over the injury which slander had done to so great a man as this, I was not a little consoled thereby. If my rivals, I told myself, could but find an equal cause for suspicion against me, with what accusations would they persecute me! But how is it possible for such suspicion to continue in my case, seeing that divine mercy has freed me therefrom by depriving me of all power to enact such baseness? How shameless is this latest accusation! In truth that which had happened to me so completely removes all suspicion of this iniquity among all men that those who wish to have their women kept under close guard employ eunuchs for that purpose, even as sacred history tells regarding Esther and the other damsels of King Ahasuerus (Esther ii. 5). We read, too, of that eunuch of great authority under Queen Candace who had charge of all her treasure, him to whose conversion and baptism the apostle Philip was directed by an angel (Acts viii. 27). Such men, in truth, are enabled to have far more importance and intimacy among modest and upright women by the fact that they are free from any suspicion of lust.

The sixth book of the Ecclesiastical History tells us that the greatest of all Christian philosophers, Origen, inflicted a like injury on himself with his own hand, in order that all suspicion of this nature might be completely done away with in his instruction of women in sacred doctrine. In this respect, I thought, God's mercy had been kinder to me than to him, for it was judged that he had acted most rashly and had exposed himself to no slight censure, whereas the thing had been done to me through the crime of another, thus preparing me for a task similar to his own. Moreover, it had been accomplished with much less pain, being so quick and sudden, for I was heavy with sleep when they laid hands on me, and felt scarcely any pain at all.

But alas, I thought, the less I then suffered from the wound, the greater is my punishment now through slander, and I am tormented far more by the loss of my reputation than I was by that of part of my body. For thus is it written: "A good name is rather to be chosen than great riches" (Prov. xxii. 1). And as St. Augustine tells us in a sermon of his on the life and conduct of the clergy, "He is cruel who, trusting in his conscience, neglects his reputation." Again he says: "Let us provide those things that are good, as the apostle bids us (Rom. xii. 17), not alone in the eyes of God, but likewise in the eyes of men. Within himself each one's conscience suffices, but for our own sakes our reputations ought not to be tarnished, but to flourish. Conscience and reputation are different matters: conscience is for yourself, reputation for your neighbour." Methinks the spite of such men as these my enemies would have accused the very Christ Himself, or those belonging to Him, prophets and apostles, or the other holy fathers, if such spite had existed in their time, seeing that they associated in such familiar intercourse with women, and this though they were whole of body. On this point St. Augustine, in his book on the duty of monks, proves that women followed our Lord Jesus Christ and the apostles as inseparable companions, even accompanying them when they preached (Chap. 4). "Faithful women," he says, "who were possessed of worldly wealth went with them, and ministered to them out of their wealth, so that they might lack none of those things which belong to the substance of life." And if any one does not believe that the apostles thus permitted saintly women to go about with them wheresoever they preached the Gospel, let him listen to the Gospel itself, and learn therefrom that in so doing they followed the example of the Lord. For in the Gospel it is written thus: "And it came to pass afterward, that He went throughout every city and village, preaching and showing the glad tidings of the kingdom of God: and the twelve were with Him and certain women which had been healed of evil spirits and infirmities, Mary called Magdalene, and Joanna the wife of Chuza, Herod's steward, and Susanna, and many others, which ministered unto Him of their substance" (Luke viii. 1-3)

Leo the Ninth, furthermore, in his reply to the letter of Parmenianus concerning monastic zeal says: "We unequivocally declare that it is not permissible for a bishop, priest, deacon or subdeacon to cast off all responsibility for his own wife on the grounds of religious duty, so that he no longer provides her with food and clothing; albeit he may not have carnal intercourse with her. We read that thus did the holy apostles act, for St. Paul says: 'Have we not power to lead about a sister, a wife, as well as other apostles, and as the brethren of the Lord, and Cephas?' (I Cor. ix. 5). Observe, foolish man, that he does not say: 'have we not power to embrace a sister, a wife,' but he says 'to lead about,' meaning thereby that such women may lawfully be supported by them out of the wages of their preaching, but that there must be no carnal bond between them."

Certainly that Pharisee who spoke within himself of the Lord, saying: "This man, if He were a prophet, would have known who and what manner of woman this is that toucheth Him: for she is a sinner" (Luke vii. 39), might much more reasonably have suspected baseness of the Lord, considering the matter from a purely human standpoint, than my enemies could suspect it of me. One who had seen the mother of Our Lord entrusted to the care of the young man (John xix. 27), or who had beheld the prophets dwelling and sojourning with widows (I Kings xvii. 10), would likewise have had a far more logical ground for suspicion. And what would my calumniators have said if they had but seen Malchus, that captive monk of whom St. Jerome writes, living in the same hut with his wife? Doubtless they would have regarded it as criminal in the famous scholar to have highly commended what he thus saw, saying thereof: "There was a certain old man named Malchus, a native of this region, and his wife with him in his hut. Both of them were earnestly religious, and they so often passed the threshold of the church that you might have thought them the Zacharias and Elisabeth of the Gospel, saving only that John was not with them."

Why, finally, do such men refrain from slandering the holy fathers, of whom we frequently read, nay, and have even seen with our own eyes, founding convents for women and making provision for their maintenance, thereby following the example of the seven deacons whom the apostles sent before them to secure food and take care of the women? (Acts vi. 5). For the weaker sex needs the help of the stronger one to such an extent that the apostle proclaimed that the head of the woman is ever the man (I Cor. i. 3), and in sign thereof he bade her ever wear her head covered (ib. 5). For this reason I marvel greatly at the customs which have crept into monasteries whereby, even as abbots are placed in charge of the men, abbesses now are given authority over the women, and the women bind themselves in their vows to accept the same rules as the men. Yet in these rules there are many things which cannot possibly be carried out by women, either as superiors or in the lower orders. In many places we may even behold an inversion of the natural order of things, whereby the abbesses and nuns have authority over the clergy and even over those who are themselves in charge of the people. The more power such women exercise over men, the more easily can they lead them into iniquitous desires, and in this way can lay a very heavy yoke upon their shoulders. It was with such things in mind that the satirist said:

"There is nothing more intolerable than a rich woman."

— (Juvenal, Sat. VI, v 459)

Chapter Fifteen - Of the Perils of His Abbey and of the Reasons for the Writing of This His Letter

REFLECTING often upon all these things, I determined to make provision for those sisters and to undertake their care in every way I could. Furthermore, in order that they might have the greater reverence for me, I arranged to watch over them in person. And since now the persecution carried on by my sons was greater and more incessant than that which I formerly suffered at the hands of my brethren, I returned frequently to the nuns, fleeing the rage of the tempest as to a haven of peace. There, indeed, could I draw breath for a little in quiet, and among them my labours were fruitful, as they never were among the monks. All this was of the utmost benefit to me in body and soul, and it was equally essential for them by reason of their weakness.

But now has Satan beset me to such an extent that I no longer know where I may find rest, or even so much as live. I am driven hither and yon, a fugitive and a vagabond, even as the accursed Cain (Gen. iv. 14). I have already said that "without were fightings, within were fears" (II Cor. vii. 5), and these torture me ceaselessly, the fears being indeed without as well as within, and the fightings wheresoever there are fears. Nay, the persecution carried on by my sons rages against me more perilously and continuously than that of my open enemies, for my sons I have always with me, and I am ever exposed to their treacheries. The violence of my enemies I see in the danger to my body if I leave the cloister; but within it I am compelled incessantly to endure the crafty machinations as well as the open violence of those monks who are called my sons, and who are entrusted to me as their abbot, which is to say their father.

Oh. how often have they tried to kill me with poison, even as the monks sought to slay St. Benedict! Methinks the same reason which led the saint to abandon his wicked sons might encourage me to follow the example of so great a father, lest, in thus exposing myself to certain peril, I might be deemed a rash tempter of God rather than a lover of Him, nay, lest it might even be judged that I had thereby taken my own life. When I had safeguarded myself to the best of my ability, so far as my food and drink were concerned, against their daily plottings, they sought to destroy me in the very ceremony of the altar by putting poison in the chalice. One day, when I had gone to Nantes to visit the count, who was then sick, and while I was sojourning awhile in the house of one of my brothers in the flesh, they arranged to poison me with the connivance of one of my attendants believing that I would take no precautions to escape such a plot. But divine providence so ordered matters that I had no desire for the food which was set before me; one of the monks whom I had brought with me ate thereof, not knowing that which had been done, and straightway fell dead. As for the attendant who had dared to undertake this crime, he fled in terror alike of his own conscience and of the clear evidence of his guilt.

After this, as their wickedness was manifest to every one, I began openly in every way I could to avoid the danger with which their plots threatened me, even to the extent of leaving the abbey and dwelling with a few others apart in little cells. If the monks knew beforehand that I was going anywhere on a journey, they bribed bandits to waylay me on the road and kill me. And while I was struggling in the midst of these dangers, it chanced one day that the hand of the Lord smote me a heavy blow, for I fell from my horse, breaking a bone in my neck, the injury causing me greater pain and weakness than my former wound.

Using excommunication as my weapon to coerce the untamed rebelliousness of the monks, I forced certain ones among them whom I particularly feared to promise me publicly, pledging their faith or swearing upon the sacrament, that they would thereafter depart from the abbey and no longer trouble me in any way. Shamelessly and openly did they violate the pledges they had given and their sacramental oaths, but finally they were compelled to give this and many other promises under oath, in the presence of the count and the bishops, by the authority of the Pontiff of Rome, Innocent, who sent his own legate for this special purpose. And yet even this did not bring me peace. For when I returned to the abbey after the expulsion of those whom I have just mentioned, and entrusted myself to the remaining brethren, of whom I felt less suspicion, I found them even worse than the others. I barely succeeded in escaping them, with the aid of a certain nobleman of the district, for they were planning, not to poison me indeed, but to cut my throat with a sword. Even to the present time I stand face to face with this danger, fearing the sword which threatens my neck so that I can scarcely draw a free breath between one meal and

the next. Even so do we read of him who, reckon-
ing the power and heaped-up wealth of the tyrant
Dionysius as a great blessing, beheld the sword secretly hanging by a hair above his head, and so
learned what kind of happiness comes as the result
of worldly power (Cicer. 5, Tusc.) Thus did I too
learn by constant experience, I who had been ex-
alted from the condition of a poor monk to the dignity of an abbot, that my wretchedness increased
with my wealth; and I would that the ambition of
those who voluntarily seek such power might be
curbed by my example.

And now, most dear brother in Christ and comrade closest to me in the intimacy of speech, it
should suffice for your sorrows and the hardships
you have endured that I have written this story of
my own misfortunes, amid which I have toiled almost from the cradle. For so, as I said in the beginning of this letter, shall you come to regard your
tribulation as nought, or at any rate as little, in
comparison with mine, and so shall you bear it
more lightly in measure as you regard it as less.
Take comfort ever in the saying of Our Lord, what
he foretold for his followers at the hands of the followers of the devil: "If they have persecuted me,
they will also persecute you (John xv. 20). If the
world hate you, ye know that it hated me before it
hated you. If ye were of the world, the world would

love his own" (ib. 18-19). And the apostle says: "All that will live godly in Christ Jesus shall suffer persecution" (II Tim. iii. 12). And elsewhere he says: "I do not seek to please men. For if I yet pleased men I should not be the servant of Christ" (Galat. i. 10). And the Psalmist says: "They who have been pleasing to men have been confounded, for that God hath despised them."

Commenting on this, St. Jerome, whose heir methinks I am in the endurance of foul slander, says in his letter to Nepotanius: "The apostle says: 'If I yet pleased men, I should not be the servant of Christ.' He no longer seeks to please men, and so is made Christ's servant" (Epist. 2). And again, in his letter to Asella regarding those whom he was falsely accused of loving: "I give thanks to my God that I am worthy to be one whom the world hates" (Epist. 99). And to the monk Heliodorus he writes: "You are wrong, brother. You are wrong if you think there is ever a time when the Christian does not suffer persecution. For our adversary goes about as a roaring lion seeking what he may devour, and do you still think of peace? Nay, he lieth in ambush among the rich."

Inspired by those records and examples, we should endure our persecutions all the more steadfastly the more bitterly they harm us. We should not doubt that even if they are not according to our deserts, at least they serve for the purifying of our souls. And since all things are done in accordance with the divine ordering, let every one of true faith console himself amid all his afflictions with the thought that the great goodness of God permits nothing to be done without reason, and brings to a good end whatsoever may seem to happen wrongfully. Wherefore rightly do all men say: "Thy will be done." And great is the consolation to all lovers of God in the word of the Apostle when he says: "We know that all things work together for good to them that love God" (Rom. viii. 28). The wise man of old had this in mind when he said in his Proverbs: "There shall no evil happen to the just" (Prov. xii. 21). By this he clearly shows that whosoever grows wrathful for any reason against his sufferings has therein departed from the way of the just, because he may not doubt that these things have happened to him by divine dispensation. Even such are those who yield to their own rather than to the divine purpose, and with hidden desires resist the spirit which echoes in the words, "Thy will be done," thus placing their own will ahead of the will of God. Farewell.

CPSIA information can be obtained
at www.ICGtesting.com
Printed in the USA
LVHW011826140720
660691LV00012B/1124